Editor
Jenni Corcoran, M.Ed.

Illustrator
Renée Christine Yates

Editorial Project Manager
Mara Ellen Guckian

Cover Artist
Denise Bauer

Managing Editor
Ina Massler Levin, M.A.

Creative Director
Karen J. Goldfluss, M.S. Ed.

Art Production Manager
Kevin Barnes

Art Coordinator
Renée Christine Yates

Imaging
Rosa C. See

Publisher

Mary D. Smith, M.S. Ed.

* Special thanks to Hannah and
Hope Burns for modeling each
pose represented in this book.

Pre-K through K

Movement Activities A to Z

- Letter & sound recognition
- Fine & gross motor development
- Practice & review materials

Author

Holly Burns

Teacher Created Resources, Inc.
6421 Industry Way
Westminster, CA 92683
www.teachercreated.com
ISBN: 9781-4206-8757-6

© *2007 Teacher Created Resources, Inc.*
Reprinted, 2010
Made in U.S.A.

Teacher Created Resources

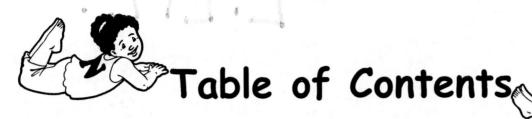

Table of Contents

Letter Units

Introduction

Young children are full of energy! Here is a resource that will assist you, the teacher, in using all the natural energy that young children possess as a vehicle to learn and retain basic skills. Movement Activities A–Z was designed to provide your students with an innovative, hands-on, multi-sensory approach to learning the letters of the alphabet and their sounds. This book is based on the following premises:

- Movement is an integral part of brain development.

- Integrating movement into existing curriculum promotes exercise as a healthy habit, while at the same time helping to cement basic skills and phonemic information into memory.

- Learning activities should center around the development of the whole child and a variety of learning styles.

- Young children learn by doing. Children retain 70–100% of the information they are taught when they hear it, see it, say it, and, most importantly, do it! Participation in learning is key.

- Repetition and frequent review of skills are important. Children need repeated exposure to skills for better retention.

- Children are able to learn new material more easily and they remember it longer when learning is fun!

How to Use This Book

There are many different approaches and curricula for teaching the alphabet. Below are suggested ways to incorporate movement and literacy-based activities into your program.

Getting Started

Introduce each letter to your students using the following techniques:

1. Choose a letter to study. Write this letter in capital and lowercase form on chart paper large enough for the whole class to see.

2. Discuss the shape of the featured letter. Emphasize curves and straight lines. Note long and short lines. Allow children to take turns coming up and tracing over the featured letter with their fingers.

3. Direct children in writing the letter in the air with their fingers. Make sure to show them the correct formation. Again, focus on the shapes of the letters.

4. Talk about the sound that the letter makes. Brainstorm a list of words that begin with that letter. Look around the room and find more words that start with the letter. Add those words to the chart, calling out each letter as you write it. Make sure to add students' names beginning with the letter.

5. Have the children bring in pictures and/or cut out pictures from magazines of things that begin with the featured letter. Add the pictures to the chart.

6. Keep each new letter chart. Post it in your classroom as a visual cue for the children. After introducing all of the letters in the alphabet, bind the letter charts together into a class alphabet big book. Have the class participate in creating a cover. Place the completed big book in your reading area for individual or shared "reading" activities.

Introduce the Movement Poem and Body Movements

There is a movement poem included for each letter of the alphabet. The purpose of each poem is to review a specific letter and letter sound(s), and to learn body movements for things that begin with specific letter sounds. The poem lines have been adjusted when more than one sound is attributed to a letter. Use the corresponding pocket chart cards for each letter to post the poems in your classroom and to refer to in teaching specific body movements to your students.

Once you have chosen a letter to study, you are ready to introduce the Movement Poem for that letter. First, cut out and assemble the word cards provided for the poem. **Please note:** Many of the words for the poems will stay the same. The main words that appear in every poem can be found in the Aa unit. Use the featured letter card with the gray box for the first line of each poem when displaying the word cards. There are also letter cards in the back of the book that can be used as titles for each poem. Each letter unit after the Aa unit will include word cards for those words that need to be replaced to correspond to the letter being studied.

Post the poem somewhere where your students can see it. Read the poem to your class, pointing to each word as it is read. Then, introduce the corresponding body movements/poses. Written descriptions and pictures of each body movement are provided. Allow plenty of space for the children to move around. Have the children come up with their own words/movements for other things that begin with the letter.

How to Use This Book (cont.)

Read the Relaxation Story

The Relaxation Story can be used to help reinforce the letter sound being taught. It is also a great way to help children calm down and relax after doing the body movements or other physical activities. Get out the Relaxation Story for the letter you are studying. Direct children to lie down flat on their backs and close their eyes. Tell them to take a deep breath in and then let it out slowly. Practice the breathing a few times. Ask them to *visualize* (make a movie in their mind) and listen for words that start with the featured letter as you read the Relaxation Story aloud. After reading the story, ask children to tell you words from the story that started with the featured letter.

Make copies of each Relaxation Story that is introduced to children. Create a binder to store the A–Z Relaxation Stories.

Make the Movement Minibook

The Movement Minibook for each letter is another way to reinforce the letter, letter sound, and body movements/poses for each letter. It is also a way to introduce a variety of important early learning skills such as holding a book correctly, reading from left to right, identifying the front and back covers and the top and bottom of a page, voice print matching, and phonics. Provide each child with a copy of the Movement Minibook. Explain that it is time to review what they have been learning. Read the book. Review the body movements for each pose if necessary. Have the minibooks pre-assembled or instruct the children to assemble their minibooks by cutting along the dotted lines, putting the pages in order, and stapling the book together. Allow children to color their books. Then have students practice reading the books and doing the body movements on their own. Students should take their books home for even more practice and to show their parents what they have been learning at school.

How to Use This Book (cont.)

Tactile Letters

A full-page template is provided for each letter (uppercase and lowercase) of the alphabet. Make a copy of the Tactile Letter page for the letter being studied. Have students decorate the letter by gluing, and/or stamping small objects beginning with the letter sound on the letter. See the list below for ideas:

A—apple prints, apple stickers

B—beans, buttons, blue things

C—cotton, candy, corn

D—dots, dinosaur stickers

E—eggshells

F—feathers, fingerprints

G—glitter, goldfish crackers

H—hearts

I—ink prints

J—jellybeans

K—key rubbings

L—leaves, licorice

M—macaroni, mosaic squares

N—noodles, nuts

O—ovals

P—popcorn, pennies

Q—quilt patches

R—ribbon, raisins

S—stickers, stars

T—toothpicks, tape

U—leave undone, upside down pictures

V—velvet, Valentine decorations

W—wool, wallpaper, gummy worms

X—draw X's (X marks the spot)

Y—yarn

Z—zebra stripes, zipper prints

Do the Cross-Curricular Activities

There are Cross-Curricular Activities included in each letter unit. These activities can be used for even more practice in large groups, small groups, one-on-one, in centers, and/or at home.

Alphabet Review Activities

After completing all of the letter units, you will find a section at the end of the book called Alphabet Review. There is a phonics review worksheet for each letter as well as Letter Cards containing each letter of the alphabet. It is suggested that you use the Letter Cards as titles for the poems as you study each letter.

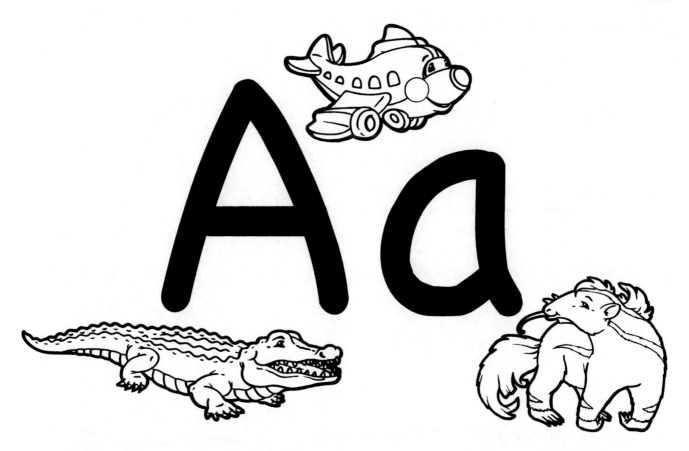

Learning the letter A can be lots of fun!

Let's try some movements, one by one!

A is for *anteater*. A is for *alligator, too!*

A is for *airplane.* Look at you!

A says "ā" or sounds like "ă." Yes, it's true.

Now let's see what you can do!

---

* There is more than one sound for the letter A. These three poses all begin with the short A sounds. Students may suggest other A words beginning with the long A sound. Perhaps you can introduce the long A with *ape* and have students act like apes.

Directions for the Letter A Poses

Anteater

1. Stand up straight and tall.

2. Stretch your arms out in front of you with your hands together to look like an anteater's long nose.

3. Move around like you are an anteater trying to catch ants.

Alligator

1. Lie down on your side making a long straight line.

2. Put your arms out over your head.

3. Move your top arm up and down like an alligator opening and closing its jaws.

Airplane

1. Stand up straight and tall.

2. Put both arms out to the sides to look like wings.

3. Move your arms up and down to look like an airplane gliding through the air.

can	be	lots
Learning	the	letter

Let's

try

movements,

of

fun!

one!

is

for

some

one

by

for

Look

at

and

too!

is

it's

true.

Now

you!

says

Yes,

you

can

do!

let's

see

what

or

sounds

like

is

for

says

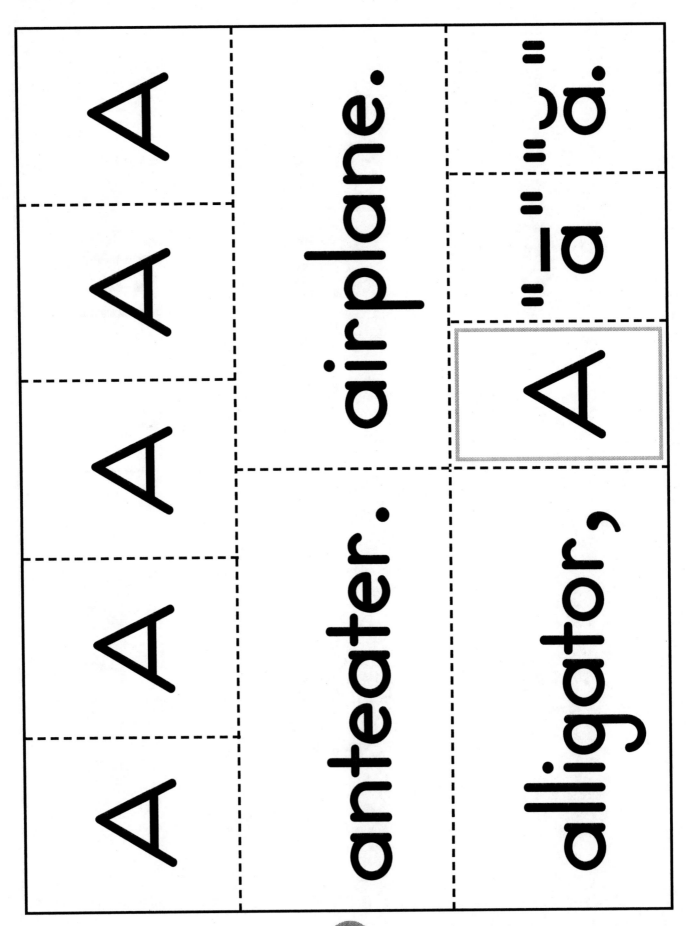

A

A

A

A

A

airplane.

anteater.

alligator,

A

anteater

anteater

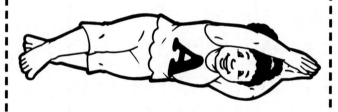

alligator

alligator

airplane

airplane

The Airplane

You are so excited! You are going on your first airplane ride. You are at the airport waiting to board the airplane. It is time to get on the airplane. You find your seat by the window, and you get ready for an amazing adventure through the sky. The airplane takes off into the air. You begin to fly higher and higher until everything below looks like ants. You close your eyes and rest for most of the ride. Now it is time to land. As you get closer and closer to the ground, you look out your window. You see some things below that begin with the sound of "a." You see apple trees and a swamp filled with alligators. You have arrived in Alabama and your Aunt Alice is waiting for you when you get off the airplane!

My Aa

Movement Minibook

A is for anteater.

1

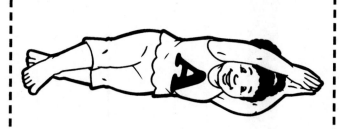

A is for alligator.

2

A is for airplane.

3

Letter A

A is for _____

20

Letter A
Cross-Curricular Activities

A is for Apples

1. Have each child bring an apple to school.

2. Sort and/or graph the apples by color.

3. Cut the apples in half and look inside for the apple star.

4. Count the apple seeds.

5. Taste the apples. Talk about different words to describe the tastes of each type of apple.

6. Use the apples to make apple prints or to make applesauce.

A is for Animals

1. Play a game of animal charades. Whisper an animal name into a child's ear.

2. Ask the child to act like that animal.

3. Allow the other children to try to guess the animal.

A is for Alphabet Soup

1. Bring to class a large cooking pot full of uncooked pasta and magnetic letters.

2. Give children metal spoons to scoop out the magnetic letters.

3. When they scoop out a letter have them identify the letter, letter sound, and/or a word that begins with the letter.

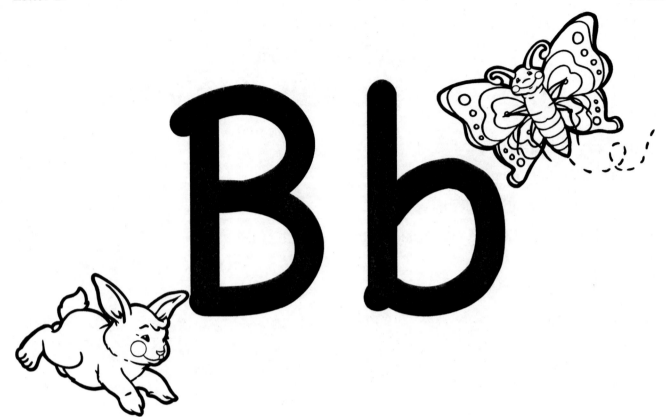

Learning the letter B can be lots of fun!

Let's try some movements, one by one!

B is for *bunny*. B is for *butterfly*, too!

B is for *boat*. Look at you!

B says "b." Yes, it's true!

Now let's see what you can do!

Directions for the Letter B Poses

Bunny

1. Stand up straight and tall.

2. Hold up your pointer fingers and place them close to your head to look like bunny ears.

3. Hop up and down like a bunny.

Butterfly

1. Sit down on your bottom.

2. Press the bottoms of your feet together with your heels close to your body.

3. Open your knees out to each side. Place your hands on your feet.

4. Move your legs up and down like a butterfly flapping its wings.

Boat

1. Sit down on your bottom with your legs stretched out straight in front of you.

2. Lift your arms up and stretch them out over your sides.

3. Then move your arms forward (toward your toes) and back (toward your chest) like you are rowing a boat.

B   B

B

boat.

"b."

B

B

bunny.

butterfly,

bunny

bunny

butterfly

butterfly

boat

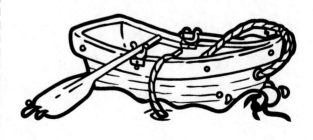

boat

The Balloon Ride

You are getting on a hot air balloon. You start to float into the air. You are going higher and higher into the sky. Oh no! You bump into a cloud. It feels so soft. As you continue to float through the air, you look down and can see a beach and many other things that begin with the sound of "b." You see a boat, a ball, a bumblebee, and a banana. You continue to float past the beach and now you see your house down below. It looks so tiny. As you get closer, it begins to look bigger and bigger. Now you are able to see into the window. You see your bed, your favorite blanket, and your teddy bear. You are tired from your balloon journey, so you land at your house. You climb into your warm bed and go to sleep. Sweet Dreams!

My
Bb
Movement
Minibook

B is for bunny.

1

B is for butterfly.

2

B is for boat.

3

Letter B

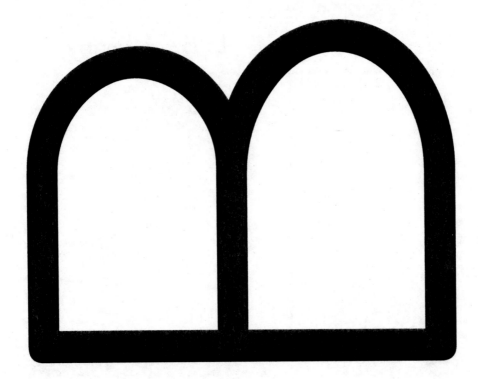

B is for _____.

28

Letter B
Cross-Curricular Activities

B is for Beanbags

1. Toss beanbags back and forth.

2. Balance and walk with beanbags on your head.

3. Play "Simon Says" by touching beanbags to different body parts.

4. Dance or march to music while balancing beanbags on different body parts.

B is for Bears

1. Have a Teddy Bear Day. Allow children to bring their teddy bears to school for the day.

2. Sing "Teddy Bear, Teddy Bear," directing children to do each of the actions with their bears.

3. Dance with teddy bears to instrumental music.

4. Decorate shoe boxes and use them to carry the bears in a "teddy bear parade."

B is for Books

1. Have a day where children bring their favorite books to school.

2. Provide time for each child to share the title of their book as well as a favorite page or part.

3. Put the books in a tub labeled "Our Favorite Books," and choose from the tub during read aloud time.

B is for Bugs

1. Fill a large tub with rice, beans, and/or sand.

2. Put a variety of plastic bugs into the tub.

3. Provide nets, jars, and magnifying glasses for children to use to dig for bugs.

4. Encourage children to sort the bugs into groups with common characteristics (e.g., green bugs, brown bugs, big bugs, little bugs, bugs with wings, etc.).

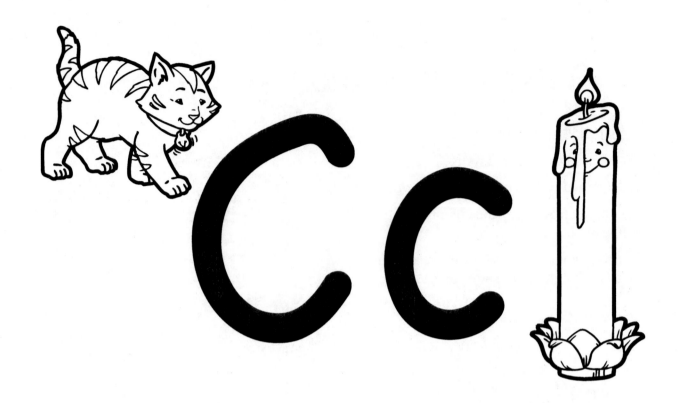

Learning the letter C can be lots of fun!

Let's try some movements, one by one!

C is for *cat.* C is for *crab*, too!

C is for *candle.* Look at you!

C says "c." Yes, it's true!

Now let's see what you can do!

Directions for the Letter C Poses

Cat

1. Get down on your hands and knees.

2. Drop your head down and arch your back.

3. As you arch your back, meow and/or hiss like a cat.

Crab

1. Sit on your bottom with your knees up.

2. Put your hands on the floor behind you and lift your bottom up off the floor as far as you can.

3. Walk like a crab using both your arms and legs to move.

Candle

1. Lie flat on your back. Place your hands under your lower back.

2. Point your toes and lift them up straight and long, pointing toward the sky.

3. Sing "Happy Birthday" while holding this pose and gently drop your legs down to "blow" out the candle.

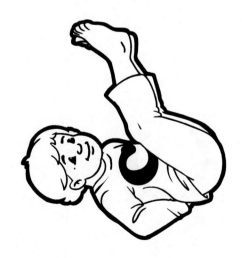

C C

C

C C

C

crab,

cat.

" "

= c.

candle.

cat

cat

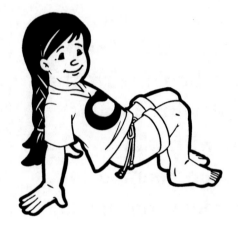

crab

crab

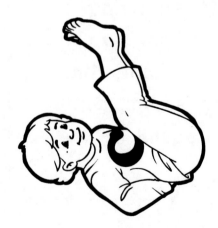

candle

candle

Clouds

It is a nice, cool spring day. You are having a picnic at the park. You just finished your lunch of carrots, crackers, and cookies. You lie down on your picnic blanket to rest. You see lots of white, fluffy clouds up in the sky. Look! The clouds look like things that begin with the sound of "c." You see a cat with a long, curly tail. You see a crab with claws. You see a caterpillar, and you can count a lot of legs. You are having so much fun making pictures out of the clouds. Soon, the clouds begin to drift away and daytime starts to turn into night. It is getting dark outside, so you decide to pack up your things and go home. You hope that tomorrow will be cloudy too, so you can make pictures in the clouds again!

My

Cc

Movement
Minibook

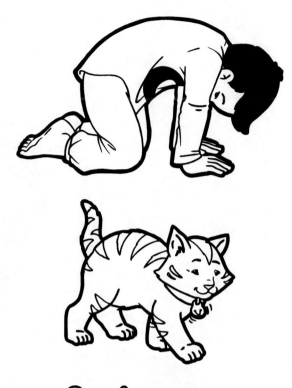

C is for cat.

1

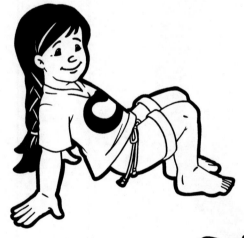

C is for crab.

2

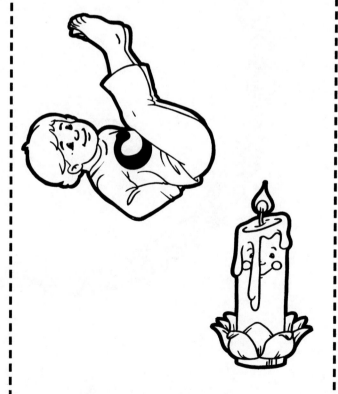

C is for candle.

3

Letter C

C is for _____

Letter C
Cross-Curricular Activities

C is for Color Collages

1. Write a color word on a large piece of construction paper.

2. Have children look for pictures of things in magazines that are that color.

3. Allow them to glue their pictures to the paper to make a color collage.

C is for Cotton Balls

1. Provide children with a large tub of cotton balls, straws, tongs, and empty egg cartons.

2. Encourage them to talk about how the cotton balls feel.

3. Allow children to blow the cotton balls with the straws, pick them up with the tongs and put them into the egg cartons, balance them on their heads, throw them in the air, and just have fun experimenting with them.

4. After experimenting, children may want to glue the cotton onto pieces of paper to make cotton ball pictures.

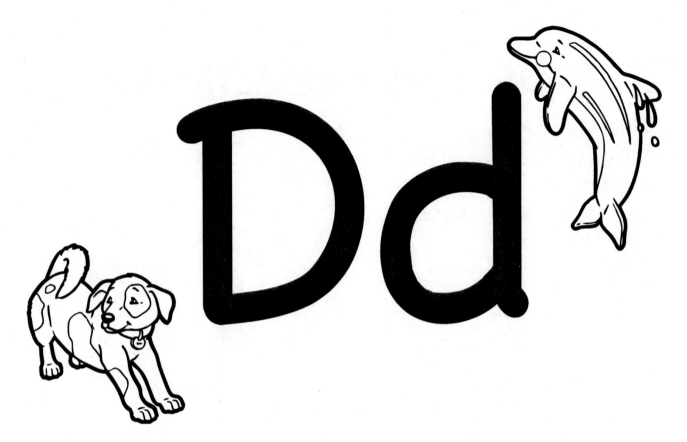

Dd

Learning the letter D can be lots of fun!

Let's try some movements, one by one!

D is for *dog*. D is for *donkey*, too!

D is for *dolphin*. Look at you!

D says "d." Yes, it's true!

Now let's see what you can do!

Directions for the Letter D Poses

Dog

1. Get down on your hands and knees.

2. Tuck your toes under and push your bottom up as high as you can.

3. Bark like a dog.

Donkey

1. Get down on your hands and knees.

2. Kick your leg up into the air like a donkey. Try to kick up your other leg, too.

3. Say "hee haw" as you kick your legs.

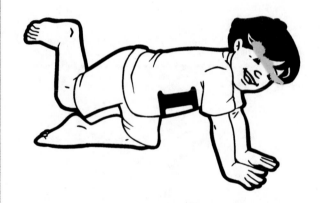

Dolphin

1. Get down on your hands and knees.

2. Put your head down on the floor with your hands on top of your head.

3. Push your back up to look like a dolphin's fin.

D D

D

D

D

donkey,

D

dog.

dolphin.

dog

dog

donkey

donkey

dolphin

dolphin

The Dream

You are very tired, so you decide to lie down and go to sleep. After you fall asleep, you start dreaming about dragons. The dragons in your dream are nice to you. The dragons teach you how to dance. They introduce you to their dinosaur friends and invite you to stay for dinner in their dungeon. A nice dragon named Dazzle takes you for a ride through the sky on his back. Down below, you see some things that begin with the sound of "d." You see a dolphin and a dog. Soon, your dragon ride comes to an end. You thank the dragons for the fun day you had together and wave goodbye. You hear a knock on your door. You wake up suddenly and realize you have been dreaming. The knock on your door is Dad. He brings you dessert and a drink!

My
Dd
Movement Minibook

D is for dog.

1

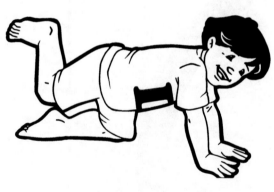

D is for donkey.

2

D is for dolphin.

3

Letter D

D is for _____

44

Letter D
Cross-Curricular Activities

D is for Dinosaurs

- Read non-fiction books about dinosaurs.

- Sort plastic dinosaurs by color, size, and shape.

- Put dinosaurs and plastic eggs in a sand or rice table, and have a dinosaur dig.

- Count and graph dinosaur-shaped fruit snacks.

D is for Dance

1. Turn on some music and dance!

2. Play the freeze-dance game. When the music starts, direct children to dance. When the music stops, direct children to freeze.

Learning the letter E can be lots of fun!

Let's try some movements, one by one!

E is for *eagle*. E is for *elephant*, too!

E is for *egg*. Look at you!

E says "ē" or sounds like "ĕ." Yes, it's true!

Now let's see what you can do!

Directions for the Letter E Poses

Eagle

1. Stand up straight and tall.

2. Put your arms together up over your head.

3. Lift up one leg and tuck it behind the other to look like an eagle perched on a branch.

Elephant

1. Stand with your legs shoulder-width apart and knees slightly bent.

2. Put your hands together. Bend your arms out in front of you to look like an elephant's trunk.

3. Walk around swinging your trunk like an elephant.

Egg

1. Sit down on your bottom with your knees bent.

2. Tuck your head down into your knees and hug your legs. Pull them in as close as you can.

3. Roll back and forth on your bottom like an egg.

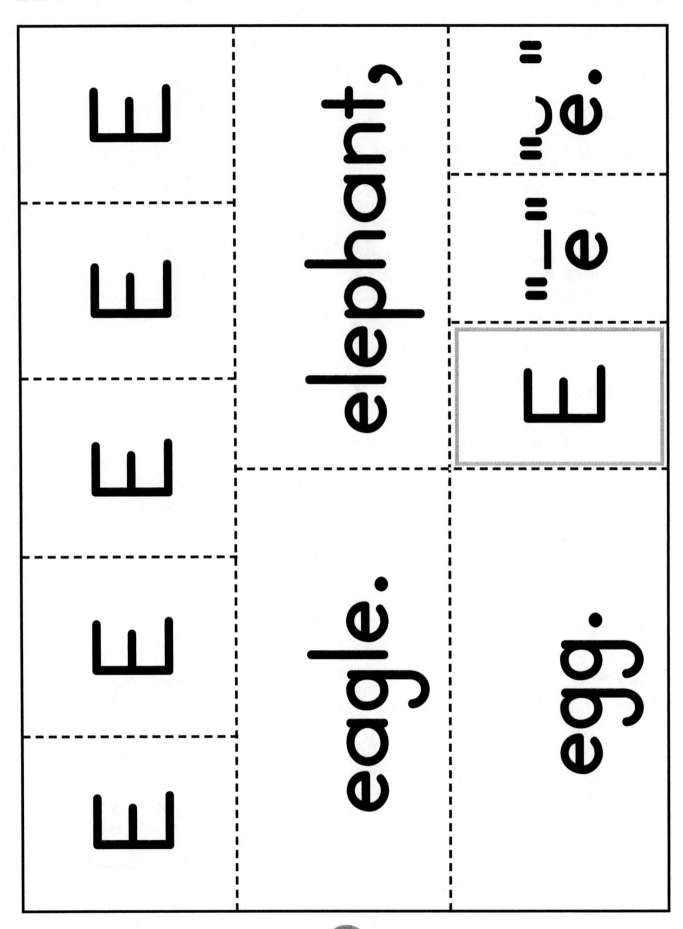

E E

E E

E E

E

elephant,

eagle.

"ē" "ē"
e

E

egg.

eagle

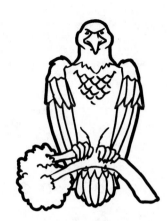

eagle

elephant

elephant

egg

egg

The Egg Hunt

You are so excited, because today you are going on an extra special egg hunt in your backyard. You open the back door, but you don't see anything except the grass, trees, rocks, and your outside toys. Where are all of the eggs? As you look closer, you see a green egg hiding in the grass. Then, you see a blue egg by the tree and a yellow one in your sandbox. You find eighteen eggs. Then, you realize that some of the eggs have treats inside that begin with the sound of "e." You find elephant stickers inside one egg and an eraser in another. Some are edible and some are empty. Each egg is a surprise. What fun! After you find all of the eggs that you can, you go inside and show your family what you found!

My

Ee

Movement
Minibook

E is for eagle.

1

E is for elephant.

2

E is for egg.

3

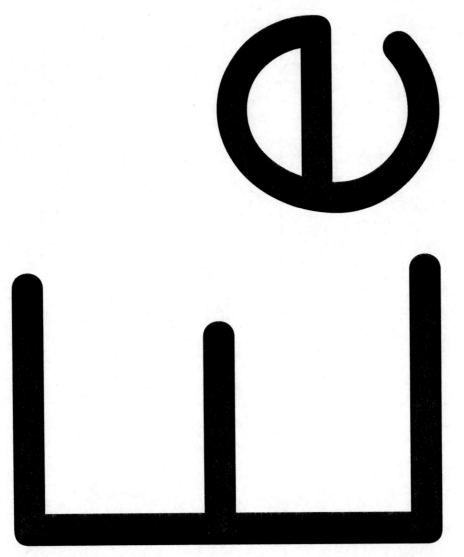

Letter E

E is for _____

52

Letter E
Cross-Curricular Activities

E is for Eggs

- Read books about animals that hatch from eggs.

- Bring chicken eggs to class and allow children to observe as they hatch.

- Decorate an egg shape pattern.

- Dye real eggs.

- Sort, count, take apart, put together, and match plastic eggs.

- Have an egg hunt in the classroom using plastic eggs.

E is for Eagle's Eye View

1. Make binoculars by taping together two toilet paper tubes.

2. Allow students to decorate their binoculars.

3. Use the binoculars to search for things that begin with the letter E.

F f

Learning the letter F can be lots of fun!

Let's try some movements, one by one!

F is for *frog*. F is for *fish*, too!

F is for *flamingo*. Look at you!

F says "f." Yes, it's true!

Now let's see what you can do!

Directions for the Letter F Poses

Frog

1. Squat down with your legs apart and knees up and out to the sides.

2. Put your hands on the floor between your knees.

3. Hop and croak like a frog.

Fish

1. Lie flat on your back.

2. Bring your feet in close to your body while pointing your knees out.

3. Puff up your cheeks to look like a fish underwater.

Flamingo

1. Stand up straight and tall.

2. Put your arms out to the sides like they are wings.

3. Lift up one leg and try to balance on one leg like a flamingo.

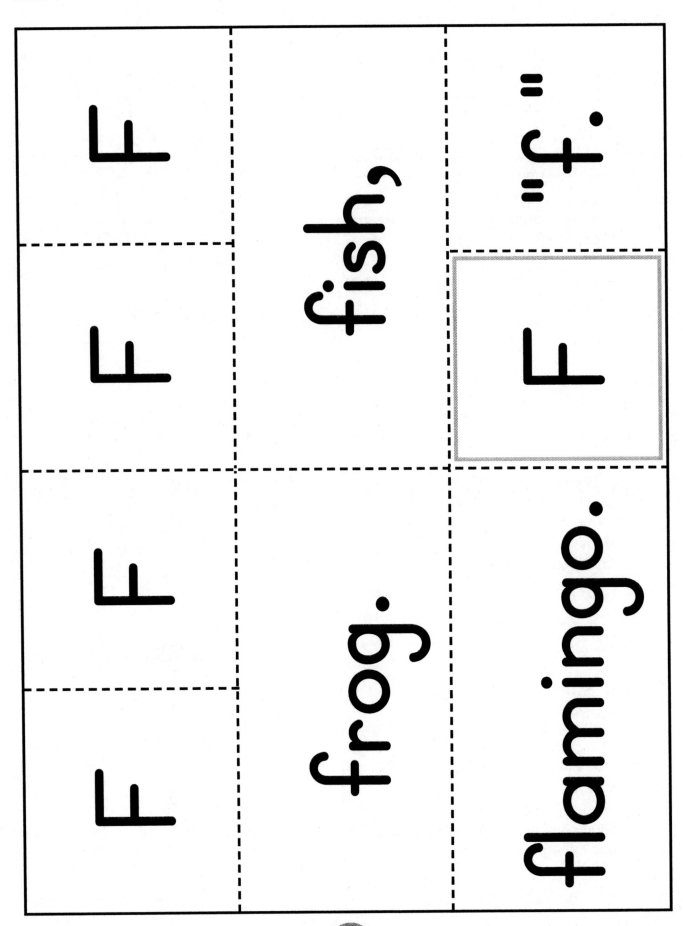

F

F

F

F

"f."

fish,

frog.

flamingo.

frog

frog

fish

fish

flamingo

flamingo

F

Floating Fun

Today is a very special day! You realize that you can float. First, you float down the stairs. Your family is surprised to see you because they didn't hear your feet. You eat some food and then you float over to feed your fish. Now, off to school. You don't want to be late, so you float very fast. On the way to school, you see some things that begin with the sound of "f." You see a frog and you see your friends. When you arrive at school, everyone has frowns on their faces. They are sad because they want to float like you. You take hold of all of your friends' fingers and let them float with you. You and your friends feel like feathers. Soon, it's time for school, so you stop floating and go inside your classroom. After school, you and your friends will have more floating fun!

My

Ff

Movement Minibook

F is for frog.

1

F is for fish.

2

F is for flamingo.

3

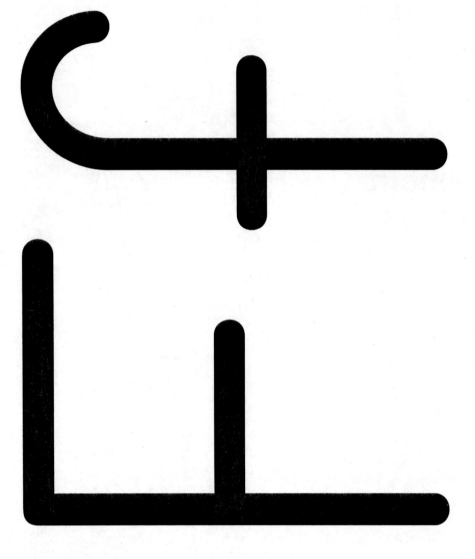

F is for _____

60

Letter F
Cross-Curricular Activities

F is for Flash Cards

1. Use index cards to make flash cards for a specific skill that you are teaching. You may want to write letters on the cards and use them for letter recognition or to have children tell you a word that begins with the letter. You may also make flash cards for number recognition.

2. As a variation, make flash cards into a matching game. Make two sets of cards, such as number cards or uppercase and lowercase letter cards. Have children match the number or letter cards together.

F is for Fishing

1. Make fishing rods out of a long dowel with a magnet attached to the end.

2. Put magnetic letters along with other water toys into the water table.

3. Allow children to fish for letters. Have them identify the letter, letter sound, and an object that starts with the letter that they "catch."

F is for Fingerprints

• Make fingerprint pictures by allowing children to put their fingers into inkpads and stamp their prints onto paper.

Learning the letter G can be lots of fun!

Let's try some movements, one by one!

G is for *gorilla*. G is for *grasshopper*, too!

G is for *giraffe*. Look at you!

G says "g" or sounds like "j." Yes, it's true!

Now let's see what you can do!

Directions for the Letter G Poses

Gorilla

1. Stand up straight and tall.

2. Make fists with your hands and bring your hands to your chest.

3. Beat your chest gently. Move around and make sounds like a gorilla.

Grasshopper

1. Squat down with your knees opened.

2. Lean forward slightly and put your arms out to the sides.

3. Hop like a grasshopper.

Giraffe

1. Stand up straight and tall.

2. Bend forward slightly.

3. Raise your arms up into the air. Stretch them up to look like a giraffe's long neck.

G G G

G G G

G G G

G G G

G G G

giraffe.

gorilla.

"." j.

"." g

grasshopper,

grasshopper,

gorilla

gorilla

grasshopper

grasshopper

giraffe

giraffe

Goggles

You are going swimming. You grab your gear and head to the pool. You are about to dive into the deep water, when you remember to get your gray goggles. You put them on, and then you get ready to dive in. One, two, three, SPLASH! When you go under the water, you look through your goggles. You can see some things that begin with the sound of "g." You see a goldfish, a goose, and giant gumballs. You take your goggles off for a minute and all the "G" things disappear. Wow! You have pretty special goggles! After a while, you get out of the pool and lay a green towel on the grass. Your goggles are beside you. While you rest, you think of all the other special things that you would like to see by looking through your goggles!

My
Gg

Movement
Minibook

G is for gorilla.

1

G is for grasshopper.

2

G is for giraffe.

3

g

68

G is for _____

Letter G
Cross-Curricular Activities

G is for Growing Grass

1. Fill small plastic cups with soil.

2. Put grass seeds in the cup, just underneath the soil. (Wheat grass seeds grow very fast. They can be purchased in most health food stores.)

3. Place the cups on a windowsill, so that they get sunlight.

4. Have children water their grass regularly.

G is for Glitter

- Provide glue and glitter for children to make sparkly designs on a large piece of construction paper.

Hh

Learning the letter H can be lots of fun!

Let's try some movements, one by one!

H is for *hummingbird.*

H is for *helicopter*, too!

H is for *house.* Look at you!

H says "h." Yes, it's true!

Now let's see what you can do!

Directions for the Letter H Poses

Hummingbird

1. Stand up straight and tall.

2. Put your hands under your armpits with elbows out to look like wings.

3. Flap your wings as fast as you can like a hummingbird.

Helicopter

1. Sit with your feet together.

2. Hold your arms out at your sides.

3. Swing your arms from side to side.

4. Make the sound of a helicopter.

House

1. Stand with your feet shoulder-width apart.

2. Bend your knees a little bit.

3. Put your arms out to the side, bending at the elbows.

"h."

H

H

H

H

house.

helicopter,

hummingbird.

hummingbird

hummingbird

helicopter

helicopter

house

house

Hiking

Put on your hiking boots. You are going on a hike through the Himalayas. You get there and see the beautiful tall mountains in front of you. Will you ever be able to make it to the top? You start your trip by hopping along the trail. As the mountains get steeper, you decide to walk instead. As you walk along the trail, you see some things that begin with the sound of "h." You see a huge rock, a hang glider, and a hippopotamus. A hippo? What is a hippo doing in the mountains? Shouldn't that hippo be in a river? You are getting hungry, so you stop to eat a hamburger. That tasted good! You start to walk again. You are almost to the top of the mountain. You are up so high. When you get to the top, you are so happy! You take a picture so you can show everyone at home!

Letter H
Cross-Curricular Activities

H is for Hats

1. Gather a bunch of hats to share with the children. Some ideas are a baseball cap, a straw hat, a crown, a top hat, a winter hat, a clown hat, a chef's hat, a firefighter's hat, a rain hat, or a shower cap. Any type of hat will work!

2. Show the hats to the children and discuss who might wear each one.

3. Display the hats in the dramatic play/dress up area for the kids to try on and play with. Have them act like the person who would wear each hat.

H is for Handfuls

1. Using the Handfuls activity page on page 78 as a template, have children take two small handfuls of a small object such as beans, pasta, or dry cereal.

2. Put one handful in each of the outlines of the hands. You may glue the objects to the paper or save the paper to reuse another time.

3. Help children to count each handful and then to fill in the blanks below by adding the two handfuls together.

Handfuls

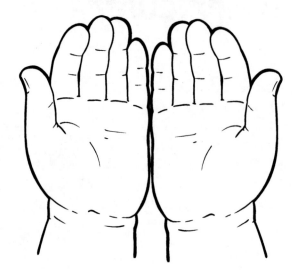

_____ + _____ = _____

Handfuls

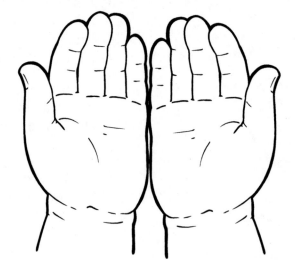

_____ + _____ = _____

Ii

Learning the letter I can be lots of fun!

Let's try some movements, one by one!

I is for *insect*.   I is for *ice skate*, too!

I is for *inchworm*.   Look at you!

I says "ī" or sounds like "ĭ." Yes, it's true!

Now let's see what you can do!

Directions for the Letter I Poses

Insect

1. Get down on your hands and knees.

2. Curl yourself up as small as you can to look like a tiny insect.

3. Put two fingers above your head to look like antennae.

Ice skate

1. Stand up with your arms out to the sides.

2. Turn your head to the left, pointing your left hand and foot out.

3. Pretend to glide on the ice like an ice skater.

Inchworm

1. Lie down on your tummy.

2. Stretch your hands over your head and make yourself as straight as you can.

3. Inch across the floor just by lifting your bottom up and down.

I

I

I

I

I

inchworm.

insect.

ĭ ī ĭ ī ĭ.

I

ice skate,

insect

insect

ice skate

ice skate

inchworm

inchworm

I

Icicles

It is wintertime. You are snuggled up warm under a blanket. Soon, you fall asleep. It starts to snow outside. You put on some warm clothes and go outside. There are icicles hanging from every rooftop. It looks incredible. You notice that the pond down the street is frozen. What a perfect day for ice skating! You go down to the frozen pond and glide across the ice on your indigo ice skates. There are other things that begin with the sound of "i" at the pond. There are people playing instruments. There are ice cream treats, too! You think it is too cold to eat ice cream! After a while, you realize that you had fallen asleep and that you must have been dreaming. You look out the window and what do you see? Icicles and ice skaters. Incredible!

My

Ii

Movement
Minibook

I is for insect.

1

I is for ice skate.

2

I is for inchworm.

3

Letter I

I is for _____

Letter I
Cross-Curricular Activities

I is for Ice Skating

1. Provide children with pieces of wax paper or paper plates to use as ice skates.

2. Direct children to put the wax paper under their shoes and slide across the floor on them.

3. Play classical music and allow them to ice skate indoors.

I is for Indian Corn

1. Give each child a cut-out of a corncob.

2. Have children glue colored popcorn kernels, popped popcorn, and/or little squares of colored paper to their corncobs.

I is for I Like Book

1. Make copies of the I Like Book.

2. Ask each child to tell you something that he/she likes for each page that is included. You may write the words for each child or help him or her write the sounds that he/she hears in each word.

3. Ask children to draw and color an illustration to match each sentence.

4. Show students how to "read" their books when they are complete.

_____'s

I Like Book

I like _____ .

I like _____ .

I like _____ .

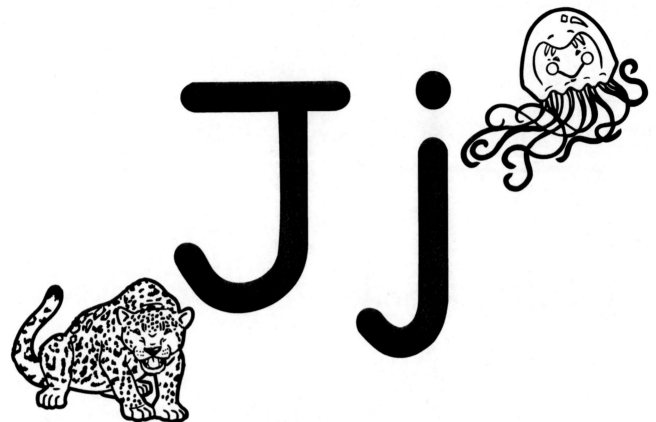

Learning the letter J can be lots of fun!

Let's try some movements, one by one!

J is for *jump rope*. J is for *jaguar*, too!

J is for *jellyfish*. Look at you!

J says "j." Yes, it's true!

Now let's see what you can do!

Directions for the Letter J Poses

Jump rope

1. Stand up straight and tall.

2. Put your arms and hands out like you are holding a jump rope.

3. Make small circle with your hands.

4. Jump up and down.

Jaguar

1. Get down on your hands and knees.

2. Lift your head and roar like a jaguar.

3. Crawl on all fours like a jaguar hunting for food.

Jellyfish

1. Sit down on your bottom with your knees up.

2. Drop your knees down to the sides.

3. Wiggle your arms like a wiggly jellyfish.

j j

j

j

j

j

jaguar,

jump rope.

jellyfish.

jump rope

jump rope

jaguar

jaguar

jellyfish

jellyfish

Jungle Journey

You are going on a journey through the jungle. You get on a jet and fly to the jungle. You jog into the tall, green trees. You can't believe how many trees, plants, and animals that you see. Oh no! You see a jaguar in the distance. You hide in a safe place until it goes away. As you continue on your jungle journey, you see some other things that begin with the sound of "j." You see a jack rabbit, a jellyfish, and a joey. This is not at all what you had expected to see in the jungle. You make a note of this in your journal, and then it is time to go. You jump aboard your jet and fly home. You tell your friends back home about the extraordinary animals that you saw on your jungle journey.

My
Jj
Movement
Minibook

J is for jump rope.   1

J is for jaguar.   2

J is for jellyfish.   3

Letter J

J is for _____

94

Letter J
Cross-Curricular Activities

J is for Jewelry

1. Provide children with pieces of ribbon, string, or yarn.

2. Have them lace straws, pasta, and/or cereal to make necklaces and bracelets.

3. Encourage them to make repeating patterns.

J is for Journaling

1. Make copies of the My Picture/My Writing activity page for each student.

2. Have children choose an event in their lives that they would like to write about.

3. Have each child draw and color a picture about that event or activity.

4. Help each student label some of the things in his/her picture by putting down the sounds he/she hears.

5. Have each child dictate a simple sentence to match the picture.

My Picture

My Writing

_____

_____

_____

_____

Kk

Learning the letter K can be lots of fun!

Let's try some movements, one by one!

K is for *kick*. K is for *kiss*, too!

K is for *kangaroo*. Look at you!

K says "k." Yes, it's true!

Now let's see what you can do!

Directions for the Letter K Poses

Kick

1. Stand up straight and tall.

2. Lift up your left leg. Hold it with your right hand and then kick.

3. Try changing sides, lifting up your right leg and holding it in your left hand before kicking.

Kiss

1. Stand up straight and tall.

2. Bring your hand to your mouth and give it a kiss.

3. Stretch your arm out straight and blow your kiss away.

Kangaroo

1. Stand up bending your knees slightly.

2. Lace your fingers together making a circle with your arms around your stomach.

3. Hop like a kangaroo.

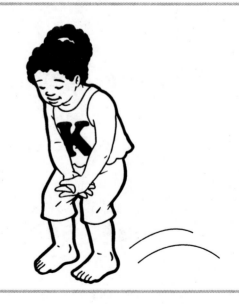

K

K

K

K

"k."

K

kiss,

kick.

kangaroo.

kick

kick

kiss

kiss

kangaroo

kangaroo

K

The Kite

It is springtime. It's windy outside so you decide to fly a kite. You hold it in the air and let the string unwind. Up, up, and up it goes high into the sky. Soon it gets stuck in a tree. You go to get it and you see that there are other things stuck in the tree that begin with the sound of "k." You see a king's crown and a kangaroo. You spot your kite, so you climb up the tree and get it down. While you are there, you take down the king's crown and the kangaroo. When you get down, you see the king. He tells you he is looking for his crown and his pet kangaroo. You give the king his crown and kangaroo. He thanks you for your kindness. You say goodbye to the king and go back to kite flying. You never thought you would meet the king while flying your kite!

My
Kk
Movement
Minibook

K is for kick.

1

K is for kiss.

2

K is for kangaroo.

3

Letter K

K is for _____

Letter K
Cross-Curricular Activities

K is for Kite

1. Have children decorate a brown paper lunch sack.

2. Punch four holes in the bottom of the sack.

3. Attach four pieces of string to the holes in the sack. Make sure the string is long enough so that the kite can float in the air.

4. Direct children to take their paper bag kites outdoors and walk quickly or run while holding them up into the air.

K is for Kings (and Queens)

1. Pretend to be kings and queens for the day. Use the Crown Pattern on page 105 as a template for making crowns.

2. Provide materials to decorate the crowns.

3. Cut them out and staple them together to fit on each child's head.

Note: Explain to children that "Queen" begins with "Q" but has a similar "K" sound.

Crown Pattern

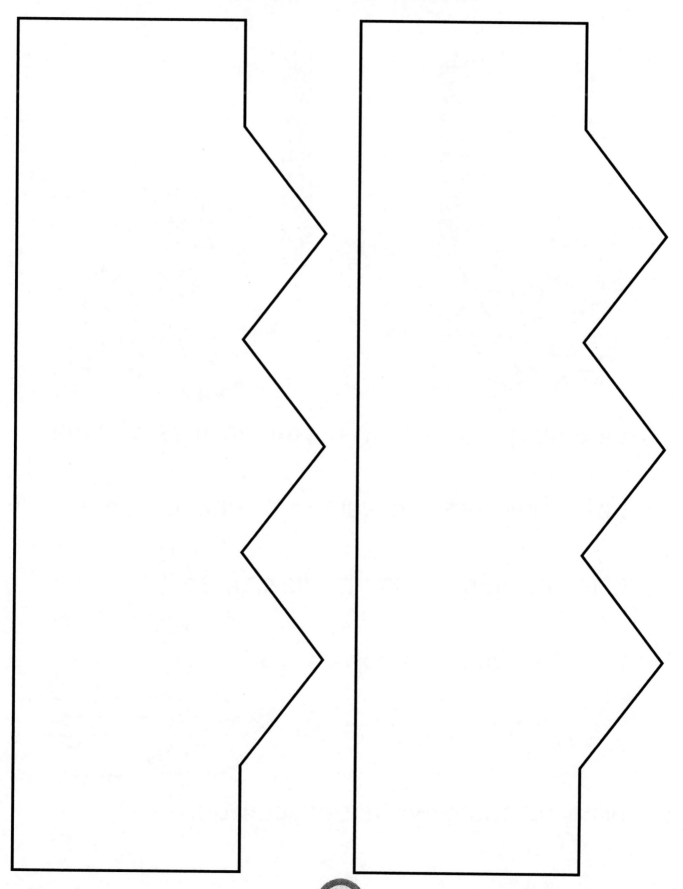

Learning the letter L can be lots of fun!

Let's try some movements, one by one!

L is for *lion*. L is for *lizard*, too!

L is for *lotus*. Look at you!

L says "l." Yes, it's true!

Now let's see what you can do!

Directions for the Letter L Poses

Lion

1. Sit down on your knees with your back straight and tall.

2. Open your knees to the sides and rest your hands on your legs.

3. Stick out your tongue and then roar like a lion.

Lizard

1. Lie down on your tummy.

2. Put your hands under your shoulders and tuck your toes under.

3. Push up until your arms and legs are straight.

4. Walk like a lizard, nice and slow, keeping your arms and legs straight.

Lotus

1. Sit on your bottom with your legs crossed.

2. Place your arms together at your chest with your elbows pointing out.

3. Raise your hands up over your head and pretend you are growing like a flower.

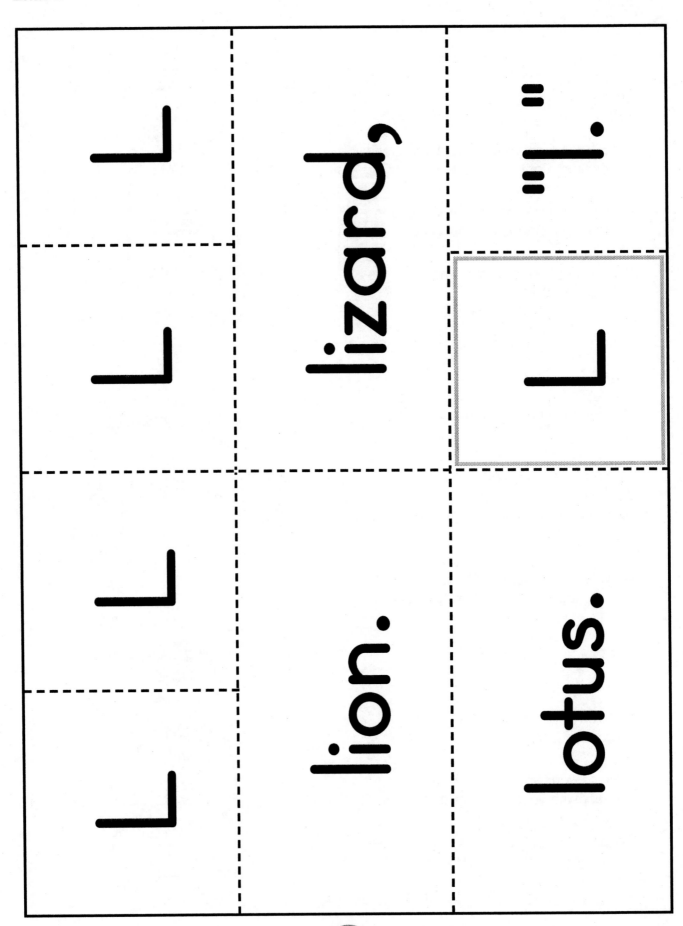

lion

lion

lizard

lizard

lotus

lotus

Lollipop Land

Today is a beautiful, sunny day, so you decide to go out and play in your backyard. When you open your back door, you notice that your backyard has turned into a lollipop land. There are lollipops where there used to be flowers and trees. There are little lollipops and large lollipops. There are lollipops of all different shapes. You see some lollipops that look like things that begin with the sound of "l." You see a lion, a lighthouse, and a leaf. They look lovely. You decide to walk out into the lollipop land and pick out a lollipop to taste. You choose one. You take a lick. It tastes like lemons and limes. Yum! You grab a handful more to take inside to share with your family. Won't they be surprised!

Letter L
Cross-Curricular Activities

L is for Letter Collections

1. Make copies of the My Letter Collection activity on page 114.

2. Write a letter in the center of the activity page.

3. Have children look for that letter in newspapers and magazines. Then, cut out and glue the letters to the paper.

L is for Leaves

1. Go outside and gather leaves.

2. Count how many leaves were collected.

3. Sort the leaves by size, shape, and color.

4. Make leaf rubbings by placing a leaf under a piece of paper and coloring on top of the paper.

My Letter Collection

Look through an old newspaper and/or magazines for the Letter _____.
Cut out any that you find and glue them in the space below.

Learning the letter M can be lots of fun!

Let's try some movements, one by one!

M is for *mouse*. M is for *monkey*, too!

M is for *mountain*. Look at you!

M says "m." Yes, it's true!

Now let's see what you can do!

Directions for the Letter M Poses

Mouse

1. Sit on your bottom with your legs crossed.

2. Put your head down inside your legs and curl up small like a mouse.

3. Squeak like a mouse.

Monkey

1. Stand up straight and tall.

2. Bend over and let your arms hang down to the floor.

3. Walk and howl like a monkey.

Mountain

1. Stand up straight and tall.

2. Put your hands by your sides.

3. Tilt your head back looking to the sky.

M

M

M

M

M

monkey,

= m.

mouse.

mountain.

mouse

mouse

monkey

monkey

mountain

mountain

The Magic Carpet

You are going shopping for new carpet with your mom. You help her pick out the most magnificent new carpet. You take the carpet home and begin to roll it out on the floor. All of a sudden, the carpet begins to move. The carpet starts to fly high up into the sky with you on top of it. Whee! You are on a magic carpet ride. It is taking you to see some things that begin with the sound of "m." You see the mountains, a monkey, and a mouse. You are having fun, but you think your mom might start to miss you. The magic carpet starts to go back in the direction of your house. It lands back on the floor. Mom decides she does not like the carpet, but you ask her to keep it anyway! She agrees, and you are looking forward to another magic carpet ride tomorrow!

My
Mm

Movement
Minibook

M is for mouse.

1

M is for monkey.

2

M is for mountain.

3

Me Book Sentence Strips

This is me.

I am _____ years old.

My birthday is _____ .

This is my family.

This is my house.

These are my friends.

This is my favorite color.

This is my favorite food.

This is my favorite thing to do.

Learning the letter N can be lots of fun!

Let's try some movements, one by one!

N is for *nap*. N is for *noodle*, too!

N is for *nautilus*. Look at you!

N says "n." Yes, it's true!

Now let's see what you can do!

Directions for the Letter N Poses

Nap

1. Lie on your side.

2. Bend your arms and your knees.

3. Close your eyes, pretend to take a nap, and snore.

Noodle

1. Sit on your bottom.

2. Put your legs out straight in front of you.

3. Wiggle your legs like a spaghetti noodle.

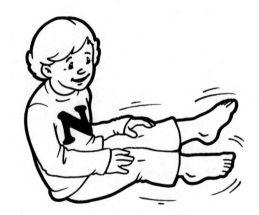

Nautilus

1. Lie on your tummy.

2. Bend your knees and lift your head back. (Try to look up, not around.)

3. Try to touch your feet to your head, curling up like a nautilus shell.

N

N

N

N

noodle,

nap.

= n.
= N

N

nautilus.

nap

nap

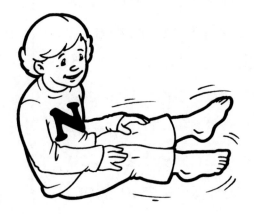

noodle

noodle

nautilus

nautilus

Nighttime

It is nighttime. It is very dark and you can see a number of stars in the sky. You count them! One, two, three, four, five, six, seven, eight, nine, ten! The stars are so neat and sparkly. After looking at the stars for a while, they start to look like pictures in the sky. Some of the pictures look like things that begin with the sound of "n." You see a nanny goat, a nest, and a net. When you look up to the North, you can see the North Star. It is the biggest, brightest star in the sky. Soon you are feeling tired, so you take a nice nap under the nighttime sky. You start to dream. You see other pictures in the sky. When you wake up, it is no longer nighttime. The stars have faded away, the sun has come out, and it is time for a brand new day!

Letter N
Cross-Curricular Activities

N is for Number Book

1. Staple together five to ten pieces of heavy paper.

2. Label each page from one to five or from one to ten.

3. Have children place the correct number of small objects into each page.

4. Make a cover for the book out of construction paper.

N is for Nests

1. Go outside and have children collect grass, sticks, leaves, and small pebbles.

2. Bring the items inside and have the children glue their items to pieces of construction paper. Suggest that the items be arranged to form birds' nests.

3. Glue large pom-poms inside for baby birds or eggs.

N is for Notes

1. Put out a variety of papers, cards, and envelopes at your writing center and encourage children to write notes to friends and family.

2. Make it even more fun by putting out a real mailbox for children to put their notes in.

3. Assign one child to be the mail carrier

Learning the letter O
   can be lots of fun!

Let's try some movements, one by one!

O is for *owl*. O is for *ostrich*, too!

O is for *octopus*. Look at you!

O says "ō" or sounds like "ŏ." Yes, it's true!

Now let's see what you can do!

---

*   There is more than one sound for the letter O. Two of these poses begin with the short O sound (ostrich and octopus) and one begins with an irregular sound (owl). Students may suggest other O words beginning with the long O sound. Perhaps you can introduce the long O with *over* and have students act out the word.

Directions for the Letter O Poses

Owl

1. Squat down with your knees apart.

2. Keep your back straight and tuck your arms behind you.

3. Turn your head slowly from side to side with eyes wide open.

4. Hoot like an owl.

Ostrich

1. Get down on your hands and knees.

2. Put your elbows down on the floor.

3. Put your knees together and lift your feet.

Octopus

1. Stand up with your legs spread apart wide, toes pointing out.

2. Bend your knees and put your hands on the floor, fingers pointing out.

3. Wiggle your fingers and toes like the tentacles of an octopus.

octopus.

owl.

ostrich,

owl

owl

ostrich

ostrich

octopus

octopus

The Ocean

It is a warm, sunny day. You are going outside for a walk on a sandy beach. When you get to the ocean, you take your shoes off. You can feel the cool, wet sand on your feet. You pick up one seashell. It is the color orange and shaped like an oval. What a special seashell. You look out into the waves and you can see some animals that begin with the sound of "o." You see an octopus and an ostrich. Wow! You continue your walk along the beach and you spot another seashell. This one is the shape of an octagon. It is getting dark now, so you turn around to make your way home. An owl swoops by. You grab a hold and the owl takes you back to where you started. Thank you owl and thank you ocean!

My

Oo

Movement Minibook

O is for owl.

1

O is for ostrich.

2

O is for octopus.

3

Letter O

O is for _____

138

Letter O
Cross-Curricular Activities

O is for O pictures

1. Provide children with pieces of construction paper, glue, and O-shaped cereal (plain and colored).

2. Have them create a design by gluing the O-shaped cereal to the paper.

O is for Opposites

1. Sing the "Opposite Song" during circle or transition times. The words follow the tune of "Do You Know The Muffin Man?" and goes as follows:

   Do you know the opposites, the opposites, the opposites?

   Do you know the opposites? Their meanings aren't the same.

   If I say big, then you say _____ .

   If I say hot, then you say _____ .

   If I say yes, then you say _____ .

   Their meanings aren't the same.

2. Stop at the blanks and allow children to come up with the opposite word.

3. Sing the song over and over again using your own pairs of opposites.

Learning the letter P can be lots of fun!

Let's try some movements, one by one!

P is for *polar bear*. P is for *pedal*, too!

P is for *pretzel*. Look at you!

P says "p." Yes, it's true!

Now let's see what you can do!

Directions for the Letter P Poses

Polar Bear

1. Lie on your tummy.

2. Open your knees and slide your feet toward your bottom.

3. Put your chin on the floor and your paws over your nose to keep warm.

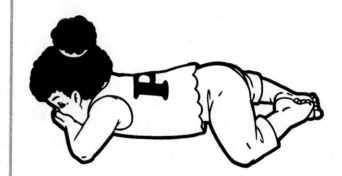

Pedal

1. Lie on your back with your hands by your sides.

2. Lift your legs up into the air.

3. Move your legs like you are pedaling a bike.

Pretzel

1. Sit on your bottom.

2. Cross your legs, one on top of the other, to look like a pretzel.

P P

P

P

pedal,

polar bear.

= =
= P.

P

pretzel.

polar bear

polar bear

pedal

pedal

pretzel

pretzel

Painting

You wake up in the morning to discover that everything around you is black or white. There is no color. You are holding a paintbrush and a palette. You decide that you will use your paint and paintbrush to paint everything pink and purple, because those are your favorite colors. You go all around your house and paint and paint and paint. You paint some things that begin with the sound of "p." You paint your pajamas and your pillow purple and some pretzels and popcorn pink. Then you decide to go to the zoo. You paint the penguins purple and the polar bears pink. You are so proud of your painting! You start to feel tired from all that painting so you go to sleep. When you wake up, everything is back to its regular color.

My

P p

Movement
Minibook

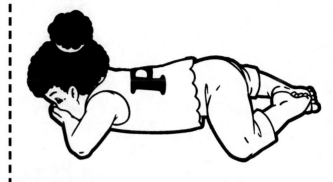

P is for polar bear.

1

P is for pedal.

2

P is for pretzel.

3

P is for ___

Letter P
Cross-Curricular Activities

P is for Pots and Pans Band

1. Give children an assortment of pots, pans, and spoons from the kitchen.

2. Turn on some music and have them march around the room playing their pot and pan instruments.

P is for Placemats

1. Make placemats by having children decorate 9" x 13" pieces of construction paper. This is especially fun to do for holidays and seasons.

2. Make sure to laminate the placemats so messes can be wiped clean.

P is for Puzzles

1. Make copies of the Puzzle Page activity on page 148.

2. Have children make their own puzzles by drawing and coloring a picture on the Puzzle Page activity (page 148).

3. After drawing and coloring their puzzles, cut them out and store them in plastic baggies or envelopes.

4. Have children switch puzzles with friends and try to put different puzzles together.

Puzzle Page

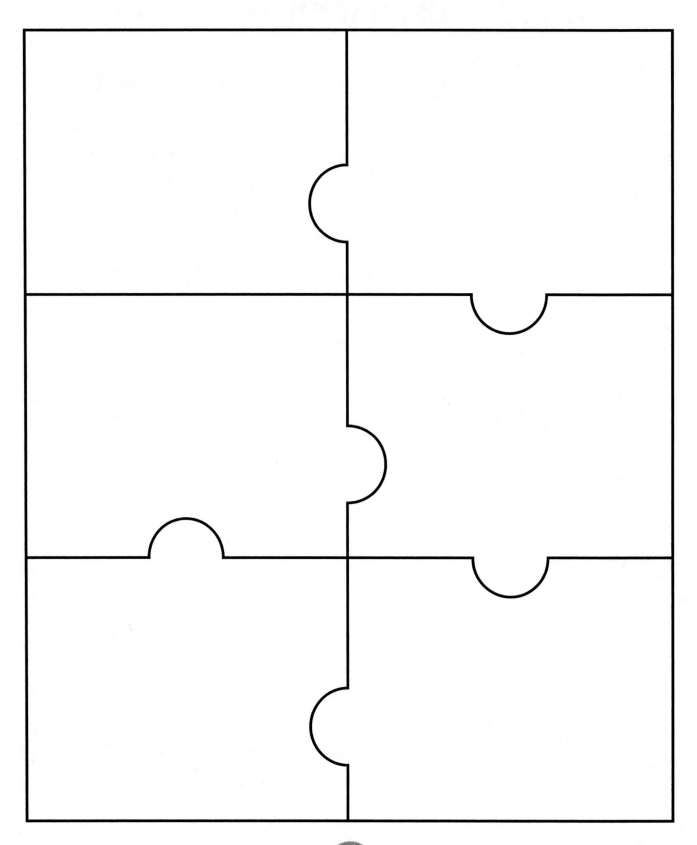

Learning the letter Q can be lots of fun!

Let's try some movements, one by one!

Q is for *quack*. Q is for *quail*, too!

Q is for *quiet*. Look at you!

Q says "qu." Yes, it's true!

Now let's see what you can do!

Directions for the Letter Q Poses

Quack

1. Stand up straight and tall.

2. Put your hands together in front of your mouth to look like a duck's bill.

3. Open and close your bill and quack like a duck.

Quail

1. Squat down with your knees pointed out.

2. Put your hands together above your head, pointing to the sky.

3. Move like a quail. Bob your head up and down and pretend to be finding seeds on the ground.

Quiet

1. Stand up.

2. Put your finger to your mouth while whispering, "Shhhh."

3. Walk quietly around the room.

| Q | quail, | =
qu.
= |
Q		Q
Q	quack.	quiet.
Q		

quack

quack

quail

quail

quiet

quiet

Quiet Time

Today you decide you want to have a quiet, relaxing, and peaceful day. You want stay in your bed with your pillow and blanket, and you want to rest. You can't wait to drift off to see what wonderful things you will dream. You dream of things that begin with the sound of "qu." You dream about a queen who has a quail. She keeps asking you questions. She wants you to answer quickly, but you just want to enjoy your quiet time. Then a duck starts quacking and quacking. The quacking wakes you up, and then it is quiet again. You continue to rest in your quiet room. As you start to drift off to sleep again, you hope that you will dream of something a little more relaxing this time!

My
Qq
Movement Minibook

Q is for quack.   1

Q is for quail.   2

Shhhh

Q is for quiet.   3

Letter Q

Q is for _____

Letter Q
Cross-Curricular Activities

Q is for Quilt

1. Make copies of the My Quilt Pattern activity on page 157.

2. Encourage children to color their quilt squares using a pattern.

3. After their quilt squares are colored, have children cut them out.

4. Assemble them together to make one big quilt and hang it on the classroom wall.

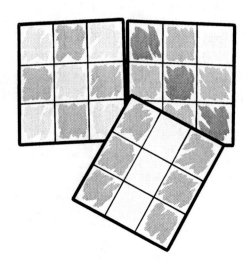

Q is for Quicksand

1. For a fun sensory experience, make quicksand using the following recipe:

Materials
- Cornstarch
- Water
- Plastic Bowl
- Spoon

Procedure

1. Put the cornstarch into the bowl.

2. Add water and stir with a spoon until it makes a smooth paste.

2. Advise students to pretend the mixture is quicksand.

3. Try rolling it into a ball. Discuss what happens.

4. Put your hand flat on the surface. Discuss what happens.

5. Poke fingers into the mixture. Discuss what happens.

My Quilt Pattern

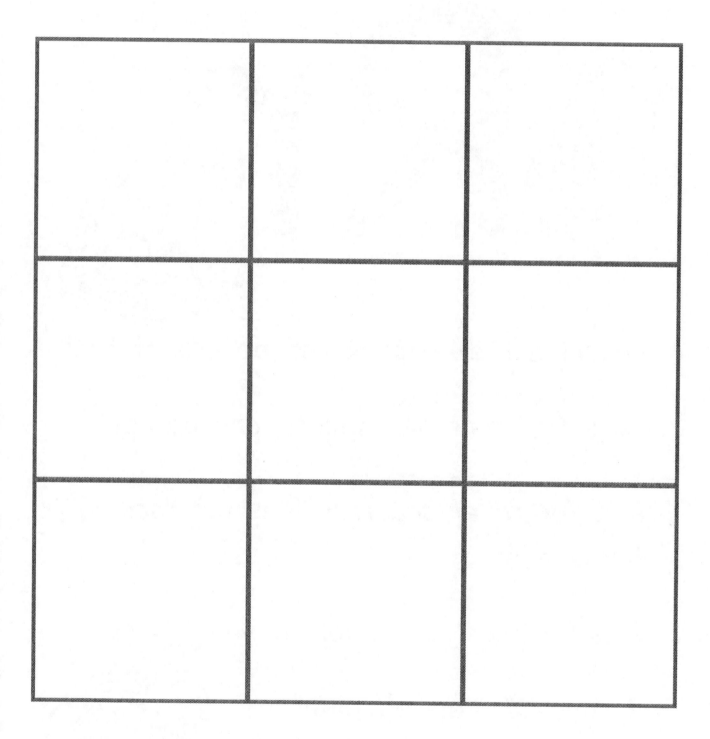

Learning the letter R can be lots of fun!

Let's try some movements, one by one!

R is for *roller coaster.* R is for *rocking horse,* too!

R is for *race car.* Look at you!

R says "r." Yes, it's true!

Now let's see what you can do!

Directions for the Letter R Poses

Roller Coaster

1. Sit down on the floor with your knees up.

2. Raise your hands up above your head like you are riding a fast roller coaster.

3. Move your hands from side to side while saying, "Wheeee."

Rocking Horse

1. Lie on your tummy.

2. Reach back with your arms and try to hold your feet in your hands.

3. Try to rock back and forth on your tummy.

Race Car

1. Sit on your bottom with your legs out straight in front of you.

2. Put your arms out and pretend you are holding a steering wheel.

3. Steer your car with your hands.

4. Make the sound of a fast race car as you pretend to drive.

R r.

R R

R R

R R

rocking horse, race car.

roller coaster.

roller coaster

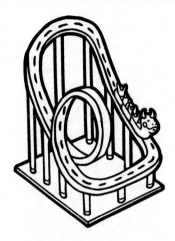

roller coaster

rocking horse

rocking horse

race car

race car

Reading

It is a rainy day, and you are reading your favorite book. The book is filled with all kinds of stories about your favorite things. You are reading stories about things that begin with the sound of "r." You read about rabbits, rattlesnakes, and race cars. When you read the story about the race car, you are suddenly in the story. You are racing in a red race car. You step on the gas and go really, really fast around the track. You go 'round and 'round. You win the race. That was radical! Suddenly you are back in your room, relaxing and reading. You start to read a story about a roller coaster ride. You hope the story will really take you there, too!

My
Rr

Movement
Minibook

R is for roller coaster. 1

R is for rocking horse. 2

R is for race car. 3

Letter R

R is for _____

164

Letter R
Cross-Curricular Activities

R is for Rhyming Word Concentration

1. Make copies of the Rhyming Word Cards on pages 166–167.

2. Cut out the rhyming word cards and lay them out face down.

3. Show children how to turn over two cards to see if they rhyme. If they rhyme, you have made a match. If not, then turn the cards back over in their original locations.

4. Group children in pairs or small groups and provide each group with a set of rhyming word cards.

5. Allow them to play the rhyming word concentration game together.

R is for Rainbow Art

1. Provide children with coffee filters and several cups of colored water.

2. Have them fill eye droppers with the colored water. Drop the colored water out onto the coffee filters. The water will be absorbed and the colors will mix together, making new colors, almost like tie-dye.

3. Discuss the new colors that appear when two colors are mixed together, like red and blue making purple.

Rhyming Word Cards

cat

hat

bee

tree

sock

rock

mouse

house

Rhyming Word Cards *(cont.)*

star

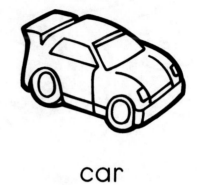

car

bug

rug

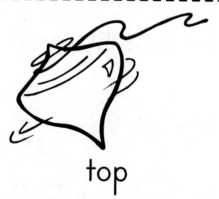

top

mop

net

jet

Learning the letter S can be lots of fun!

Let's try some movements, one by one!

S is for *stork*. S is for *snake*, too!

S is for *star*. Look at you!

S says "s." Yes, it's true!

Now let's see what you can do!

Directions for the Letter S Poses

Stork

1. Stand up straight and tall.

2. Lift one arm up and curve your hand below your chin to look like a beak.

3. Bend the opposite knee, lifting up your foot.

4. Look straight ahead at something that is not moving. This will help you balance.

Snake

1. Lie on your tummy.

2. Put your hands flat on the floor and lift your chest and head up.

3. Hiss like a snake.

Star

1. Sit on your bottom with your knees out, and the bottoms of your feet touching.

2. Bend over and touch your head to the floor.

3. Put your hands on the back of your head.

S

S

S

S

snake,

stork.

"s."

S

star.

stork

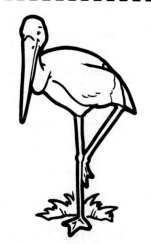

stork

snake

snake

star

star

The Spaceship

Put on your spacesuit, get inside your rocket ship, and buckle up. You are going on a trip into outer space. Countdown to blast off.

10, 9, 8, 7, 6, 5, 4, 3, 2, 1. Blast off!

Up, up, and up you go, past the clouds and into outer space. You are going so fast! When you look out your window, you can see things that begin with the sound of "s." You see so many stars. You see seven space rocks. Soon, you land on the planet Saturn. You get out of your spaceship. You are the first person to step on Saturn. Saturn feels like sand. You skip and slide all around. It is like playing in a gigantic sandbox. You are having a super time, but you know you must get back home soon. You get back into your spaceship and fly back to Earth.

Letter S
Cross-Curricular Activities

S is for Spiral Snake

1. Make copies of the Spiral Snake activity on page 176.

2. Provide safety scissors for the children. Direct them to cut on the bold lines.

3. You can also have children decorate the undersides of their snakes. Hang them from the ceiling.

S is for Shaving Cream

1. For a fun sensory experience, put down pieces of wax paper for each child.

2. Put a small amount of shaving cream on each piece of wax paper.

3. Direct children to use the shaving cream to draw pictures and practice writing letters or words. They can use their fingers, rounded tooth picks, or cotton swabs to draw in the shaving cream.

S is for Shape Designs

1. Provide children with a large piece of construction paper and a variety of pre-cut shapes, including squares, circles, rectangles, and triangles.

2. Allow them to glue the shapes to their papers to make designs.

3. Later, encourage children to make the shapes look like a real object such as an animal, a boat, or a person.

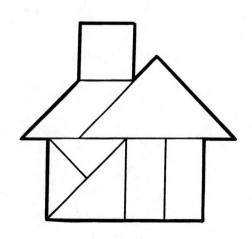

Spiral Snake

Begin cut here.

Learning the letter T can be lots of fun!

Let's try some movements, one by one!

T is for *tree*. T is for *triangle*, too!

T is for *teapot*. Look at you!

T says "t." Yes, it's true!

Now let's see what you can do!

Directions for the Letter T Poses

Tree

1. Stand up straight and tall.

2. Put your hands up over your head to look like tree branches.

3. Lift up one of your feet and put it on the other knee.

Triangle

1. Stand up with your legs spread apart.

2. Put your arms out to the sides.

3. Bend over to one side touching your hand to your foot.

4. Put the other arm up in the air, pointing to the sky.

Teapot

1. Stand up with your legs spread apart.

2. Bend one arm to make a handle for your teapot.

3. Put your other arm up with your hand bent to make the spout for your teapot.

4. Bend over, using the side that is the spout to pour out some tea.

T

triangle,

"t."

T

T

T

tree.

teapot.

T

tree

tree

triangle

triangle

teapot

teapot

T

Travel Through Time

You are playing in your tree house when it starts to shake, spin, and fly through the air. Soon it lands, and you look out a tiny window. You have traveled through time, back to the age of the dinosaurs. You can see some dinosaurs that start with the sound of "t." You see a Triceratops and a Tyrannosaurus Rex. You are a little afraid, but you get out of your tree house anyway. You put out your hand to touch the dinosaurs. Whew! They are nice dinosaurs. They can talk, too! They invite you to tea. You spend the afternoon drinking tea together. No one is ever going to believe this! You get back into your tree house. It starts to move again. I wonder where you are going this time?

My
T t

Movement
Minibook

T is for tree.

1

T is for triangle.

2

T is for teapot.

3

Letter T

T is for _____

183

Letter T
Cross-Curricular Activities

T is for Transportation

1. Set up a Transportation Station in your classroom to be used at Center Time. Provide all different kinds of play vehicles, such as airplanes, cars, trucks, boats, and bikes.

2. Encourage children to tell you which ones travel by land, water, and air.

3. Allow children to paint with toy cars. Just dip the wheels in paint and "drive" the cars on the paper.

The Three Bears

1. Read the story of "Goldilocks and The Three Bears."

2. Practice retelling the story by using stuffed animals and/or puppets to act it out.

3. Make place settings for the three bears, using bear stuffed animals, plates, cups, and silverware.

4. Practice counting by threes.

5. Brainstorm a list of other things that come in threes.

- Three Men in a Tub
- Three Blind Mice
- three wheels on a tricycle
- three corners on a triangle

Learning the letter U can be lots of fun!

Let's try some movements, one by one!

U is for *umbrella*. U is for *unicorn*, too!

U is for *upside down*. Look at you!

U says "ū" or sounds like "ŭ."
Yes, it's true!

Now let's see what you can do!

Directions for the Letter U Poses

Umbrella

1. Stand up with your legs spread apart.

2. Spread your arms out above your head.

3. Do jumping jacks and pretend to be an umbrella that is opening and closing.

Unicorn

1. Sit down on your knees.

2. Lean forward a little bit, keeping your back straight.

3. Put your hands together and place them on top of your head to look like a unicorn's horn.

Upside Down

1. Stand up with your legs spread apart.

2. Bend over and put your hands on the floor.

3. Look through your legs.

U

U

U

U

U

umbrella.

unicorn,

u="=,
u=,=
u.

upside down.

umbrella

umbrella

unicorn

unicorn

upside down

upside down

U

Underwater

Put on your scuba gear. Get ready for an underwater adventure. Ready, set, splash! You are underwater. You dive deeper and deeper. It is so beautiful. You see a coral reef and many different underwater animals! You spot a sunken ship, so you swim inside to check it out. Inside the ship, you see some things that begin with the sounds of "ū" and "ŭ." You see an umbrella, a unicycle, and a picture of a unicorn. You wonder what these things are doing in the ship. Maybe the ship had been traveling to the circus. You continue on your underwater adventure. Some sea urchins have made a home on a ukelele that must have fallen off a ship. You are amazed at all the unbelievable things that you see!

My U u

Movement Minibook

U is for umbrella.

1

U is for unicorn.

2

U is for upside down.

3

Letter U

U is for _____ •

Letter U
Cross-Curricular Activities

U is for Unit Cubes

- Sort unit cubes by color.

- Use unit cubes to count.

- Use unit cubes to measure different things around the classroom.

- Link unit cubes to make patterns.

- Use unit cubes and a balance scale to see how many cubes weigh as much as another object.

U is for Utensils

1. Fill a large tub with sand, water, rice, beans, and/or packaging materials.

2. Provide children with different utensils and containers to use for scooping, filling, pouring, and measuring.

Learning the letter V can be lots of fun!

Let's try some movements, one by one!

V is for *volleyball*. V is for *volcano*, too!

V is for *vulture*. Look at you!

V says "v." Yes, it's true!

Now let's see what you can do!

Directions for the Letter V Poses

Volleyball

1. Stand up with your legs spread apart.

2. Lace your fingers together with your arms straight and pressing against your body.

3. Lift your arms up like you are going to hit a volleyball.

Volcano

1. Stand up with your legs spread wide apart.

2. Reach up and out, pretending that you are an erupting volcano.

3. Make a rumbling sound.

Vulture

1. Stand with your legs apart and knees slightly bent.

2. Put your arms out to the sides with your elbows and hands bent.

3. Stay perched or straighten your wings and pretend to soar through the air.

V

V

V

V

V

vulture.

volcano,

volleyball.

= =
v.
= =

volleyball

volleyball

volcano

volcano

vulture

vulture

Video Game

You are playing your favorite video game, when all of a sudden you are *in* the video game. You are wearing a special velvet vest. A vulture swoops down and picks you up and carries you through the air. Down below, you can see something that starts with the sound of "v." It is a volcano. You must stop the volcano from erupting. Oh, no! The lava is coming out of the volcano. You push a button on your velvet vest, and the lava stops. You are safe. You want to get out of the video game. You push another button on your velvet vest, and you are back in your room playing your video game. You decide to play another game. In the new game, you are swinging on a giant vine. Below, you see vegetables dancing.

My

Vv

Movement
Minibook

V is for volleyball.

1

V is for volcano.

2

V is for vulture.

3

Letter V

V is for _____

Letter V
Cross-Curricular Activities

V is for Valentines

- Allow children to make Valentine's any time of year. Provide supplies to decorate the valentines.

- Put pre-made Valentine cards at the writing center for children to write.

- Show children how to cut hearts out of paper by folding a piece of paper in half and cutting out one side of the heart. Then open the paper up and you have a heart.

V is for Volcano

Materials

- Clay or playdough

- baking soda

- vinegar

1. Make a volcano out of playdough or modeling clay.

2. Make a large crater in the top.

3. Put 1 tablespoon baking soda in the crater. Then, pour 1 tablespoon vinegar into the crater.

4. Watch the volcano erupt!

Learning the letter W can be lots of fun!

Let's try some movements, one by one!

W is for *walrus*. W is for *wagon*, too!

W is for *windmill*. Look at you!

W says "w." Yes, it's true!

Now let's see what you can do!

Directions for the Letter W Poses

Walrus

1. Lie down on your tummy.

2. Arch your back and lift your head.

3. Put your hands below your chin to make tusks.

Wagon

1. Lie down on your back.

2. Place your hands under your lower back.

3. Raise both feet to the sky, keeping your legs as straight as you can.

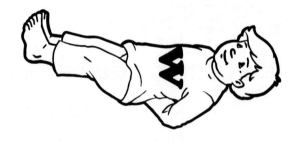

Windmill

1. Stand up with your legs spread apart.

2. Put both hands on the floor in front of you.

3. Raise one arm up, pointing to the sky, while leaving the other flat on the floor.

W

W

W

W

W

windmill.

walrus.

w. =
=

wagon,

walrus

walrus

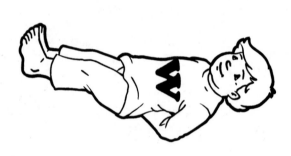

wagon

wagon

windmill

windmill

W

The Wishing Wand

You find a weird looking wooden box in your room. You open it up, and inside there is a magic wand. You take the magic wand out of the box. It has a tag on it that says, "Good for three wishes." You wave the wand in the air and make a wish. You wish for something that begins with the sound of "w." You wish you could go for a ride on a whale down a waterfall. Suddenly, you are riding on a whale and you are going down a big waterfall. Whee! Splash! That was wonderful! You wave your wand and make another wish. You wish you could go to a winter wonderland. All of a sudden, you are in a winter wonderland. Wow! You make your final wish . . . that you can have as many wishes as you want. What will you wish for next?

Good for three wishes

My

Ww

Movement
Minibook

W is for walrus.　1

W is for wagon.　2

W is for windmill.　3

Letter W

W is for _____

207

Letter W
Cross-Curricular Activities

W is for Watermelon Math

1. Use a piece of string to estimate and measure the circumference of a watermelon.

2. Weigh a watermelon.

3. Estimate how many seeds will be inside a watermelon.

4. Cut it open and count the seeds.

5. Don't forget to taste the watermelon!

W is for Weather Watching

1. Make copies of the Weather Chart activity on page 209.

2. Keep track of the weather as a class, or have children do it at home.

Weather Chart

Draw a picture of what kind of weather you see each day.

Monday	Tuesday
Wednesday	**Thursday**
Friday	**Weekend**

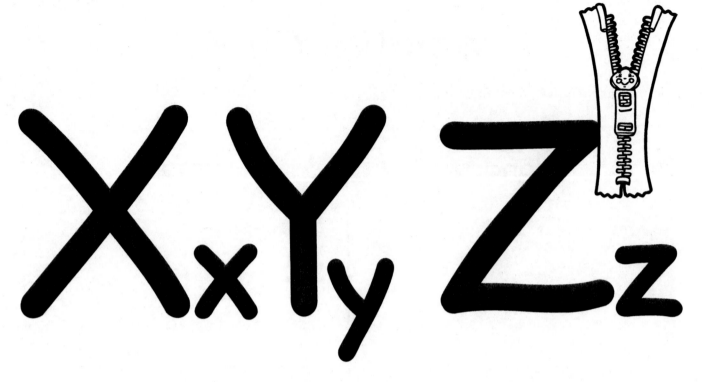

Learning the letters X, Y, and Z can be lots of fun!

Let's try some movements, one by one!

X is for *x-ray fish.* Y is for *yak, too!*

Z is for *zipper.* Look at you!

X says "x." Y says "y." Z says "z." Yes, it's true!

Now let's see what you can do!

Directions for the Letters X,Y,Z Poses

X-ray Fish

1. Lie on your back.

2. Open your arms and legs out wide to the sides.

Yak

1. Sit up on your knees, with your back straight.

2. Cup your hands, and put them facing out on your head to look like a yak's horns.

Zipper

1. Lie on your back.

2. Bend your elbows and your knees.

3. Try to put the bottoms of your feet together.

4. Pretend to zip and unzip by straightening and bending your legs.

Y.

Z.

x.

Z

Y

X

x-ray fish.

zipper.

yak, says

x–ray fish

x–ray fish

yak

yak

zipper

zipper

XYZZZZZ's

It is bedtime. You yawn and slowly drift off to sleep. Suddenly, you are at one of your favorite places—the zoo. You look at all of the animals. You see some animals that begin with the sound of "x," "y," and "z." You see an x-ray fish, a yak, and a zebra. You feed the animals and play with them. This is the most fun that you have ever had at the zoo. You wake with a yawn, only to realize that you were dreaming. You look beside you, and there are your x-ray fish, yak, and zebra stuffed animals. You give each one a hug and then drift back to sleep. ZZZZZZZ's! Sweet Dreams!

My

XxYyZz

Movement Minibook

X is for x-ray fish.

1

Y is for yak.

2

Z is for zipper.

3

Letter X

X is for _____

216

Letter Y

Y is for _____

Letter Z

Z is for _____.

218

Letters X, Y & Z
Cross-Curricular Activities

X is for Boxes

1. Provide different boxes with lids. Jewelry boxes, gift boxes, and shoe boxes work well.

2. Have students match lids to the boxes, stack the boxes, etc.

3. Have students stack and count the boxes.

Y is for Yellow

1. Use yellow playdough or paint to practice mixing colors together.

2. Try mixing yellow and blue to make green, or yellow and red to make orange.

3. Have the students bring in yellow foods for snacks.

Z is for Zoo

• Take a field trip to the zoo. Make a language experience chart after the field trip. Use the following sentence:

At the zoo, I saw a _____.

Have each child contribute a word to the chart.

• You could also make a class book by writing the same line at the bottom of each child's page. Have children illustrate their pages. Help them write the word for an animal they would like to see at the zoo in the blank. Bind all of the pages together into a class book.

A is for . . .

Circle and color all the things below that begin with the letter A.

- -

B is for . . .

Circle and color all the things below that begin with the letter B.

C is for . . .

Circle and color the things below that begin with the letter C.

- -

D is for . . .

Circle and color the things below that begin with the letter D.

E is for . . .

Circle and color the things below that begin with the letter E.

- -

F is for . . .

Circle and color the things below that begin with the letter F.

G is for . . .

Circle and color the things below that begin with the letter G.

- -

H is for . . .

Circle and color the things below that begin with the letter H.

I is for . . .

Circle and color the things below that begin with the letter I.

J is for . . .

Circle and color the things below that begin with the letter J.

K is for . . .

Circle and color the things below that begin with the letter K.

- -

L is for . . .

Circle and color the things below that begin with the letter L.

M is for . . .

Circle and color the things below that begin with the letter M.

N is for . . .

Circle and color the things below that begin with the letter N.

O is for . . .

Circle and color the things below that begin with the letter O.

- -

P is for . . .

Circle and color the things below that begin with the letter P.

Q is for . . .

Circle and color the things below that begin with the letter Q.

R is for . . .

Circle and color the things below that begin with the letter R.

S is for . . .

Circle and color the things below that begin with the letter S.

- -

T is for . . .

Circle and color the things below that begin with the letter T.

U is for . . .

Circle and color the things below that begin with the letter U.

V is for . . .

Circle and color the things below that begin with the letter V.

W is for . . .

Circle and color the things below that begin with the letter W.

- -

X is for . . .

Circle and color the picture below that begins with the letter X.

Y is for . . .

Circle and color the picture below that begins with the letter Y.

- -

Z is for . . .

Circle and color the picture below that begins with the letter Z.

Aa Bb

Cc Dd

Ee Ff

Gg Hh

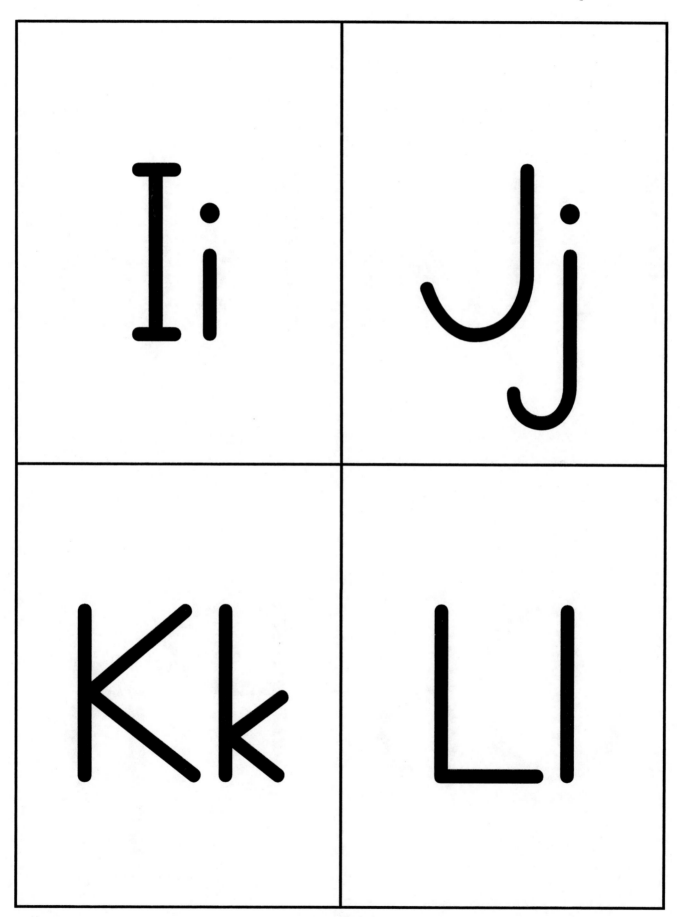

Mm Nn

Oo Pp

Qq Rr

Ss Tt

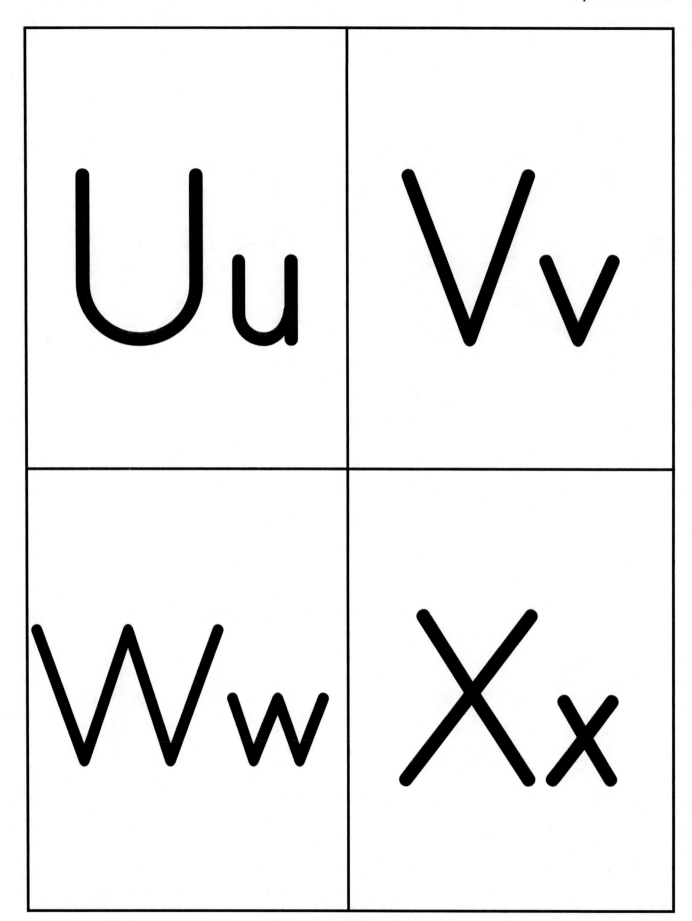

Yy

Zz

a b c d e f g h i j k l m n o p q r s t u v w x y z

 Trace the letters of the alphabet.

A   B   C   D

E   F   G   H

I   J   K   L

M   N   O   P

Q   R   S   T

U   V   W   X

Y   Z